Little White

The Feral Cat Who Found a Home

by Faye Rapoport DesPres

Illustrations by Laurel McKinstry Petersen

Stray Cat Stories
Book 1

Writer's Coffee Bar Press
New Jersey

This book is dedicated to Deborah Schreiber, who helped us rescue Little White, and the volunteers everywhere who rescue lost or stray animals.

~ Thank you!

Little White didn't have a family.

There was no one to play with her
or give her treats.

So she swatted at sticks,
raced around rocks,
and gobbled up anything
she could find to eat . . .
                even if she found it in the trash.

Little White was lonely,
and her life was hard.

One day, a new cat showed up with Little White.

They looked like twins, right down to the gray patches between their ears. The only difference was their size.

So I called them Big White and Little White.

They were shivering, and a blizzard was coming.
I had to help them, *fast!*

I covered a cat carrier with coats and put it in the yard, hoping they would crawl inside and stay warm.

When morning came,
the snow was piled high.

Big White was inside the carrier,
all alone and sitting up straight.
She looked at me as if to say, "You're late!"

Some friends came to meet her and fell in love.
They took her home and named her Snowflake.

I called for her, but she ran away.

The next morning, I heard a noise . . .
it was a coyote!

He had flashing white teeth,
and big, hungry eyes.

Little White was in danger!
I had to find a way to get her inside.

I put a bowl of food outside.

Every day, I moved the bowl a little closer to our door.

Little White was nervous, but very hungry.

As the days passed, she came closer and closer.

Finally, I put the bowl just inside the door and left it open. Little White stepped inside . . .

... and I closed the door behind her!

Love is powerful.
It can make you feel safe and strong.

Even though Little White was afraid,
she wanted to be loved.
And we wanted to love her.

Soon, she crept out of the closet
and began to explore our house.

Little White made friends with our cat, Tribbs.
He was black except for his white nose,
tummy, and dashing boots.

They were a perfect pair.
Her yin to his yang,
one light, one dark, one girl, one boy.

Little White settled into our home.
She climbed on her condo,
and played hide-and-seek with Tribbs.
She rolled on our rugs,
and napped on our pillows.

After a few weeks, Little White arched her back and let me pet her. And that's when I heard it.... Little White's purr.

Little White isn't alone anymore. She has a best friend, plenty of food, and a soft bed to sleep in at night.

...she is *our* Little White.

Copyright ©2018 Faye Rapoport DesPres

Published in the United States by Writer's Coffee Bar Press, Edison, New Jersey.

All rights are reserved. No part of this book may be reproduced or utilized in any form or by any means, electronic or mechanical, including photocopying, recording, or any information storage and retrieval systems without permission in writing from the author.

Illustrations by Laurel McKinstry Petersen
Cover and Book Layout/Design by MaryChris Bradley
ISBN 978-1-941523-16-2 (Original Paperback)
Library of Congress Control Number: 2018911058
First Paperback Edition, October 2018

Also by the author
Message from a Blue Jay: Love, Loss and One Writer's Journey Home

www.ingramcontent.com/pod-product-compliance
Lightning Source LLC
Chambersburg PA
CBHW051350110526
44591CB00025B/2960